01 PRE-SHOOT CHECKLIST

Check these settings before you head out with your camera!

SETTING	MY PREFERRED SETTING
☑ Shooting Mode	....
☑ White Balance Setting	....
☑ ISO Setting	
☑ Focus Mode	
☑ AF-Area Mode	
☑ Release Mode	
☑ Metering Mode	
☑ Bracketing: On/Off	....
☑ File Format: JPEG/HEIF, RAW, or RAW+JPEG/HEIF	....
☑ Highlight Warning: On/Off	....
☑ Vibration Reduction: On/Off/Sport	....
☑ Picture Control	....
☑ Flash Mode	....
☑ Battery Fully Charged and In Camera	....
☑ Memory Card(s) Formatted and In Camera	....

02 BUTTONS, DIALS, AND SCREENS

CAMERA BODY TOP

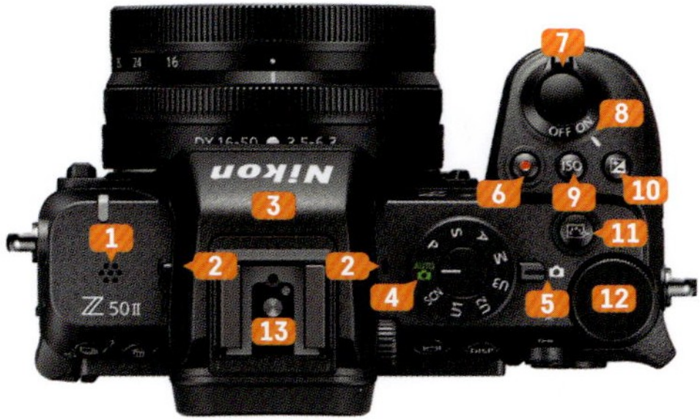

1. **Speaker:** Used for sound playback.
2. **Stereo Microphones:** Records audio when shooting video.
3. **Pop-up Flash:** Used for flash photography.
4. **Mode Dial:** Use to set the shooting mode.
5. **Photo/Video Selector:** Switches between black-and-white photo, color photo, and video modes.
6. **Video Record Button:** Starts and stops video recording when camera is set to video mode.
7. **Shutter Release Button:** Press halfway down to activate autofocus and all the way down to take a photo.

TABLE OF CONTENTS

8. **On/Off Switch:** Turns the camera on and off.

9. **ISO:** Press this button, then rotate the command dial to change the ISO.

10. **Exposure Compensation Button:** Press this button, then rotate the command dial to set the exposure compensation.

11. **Picture Control Button:** Used to set the Picture Control.

12. **Main Command Dial:** Rotate the command dial to change your settings.

13. **Accessory Shoe:** Attach external flash units or other compatible accessories here.

CAMERA BODY BACK

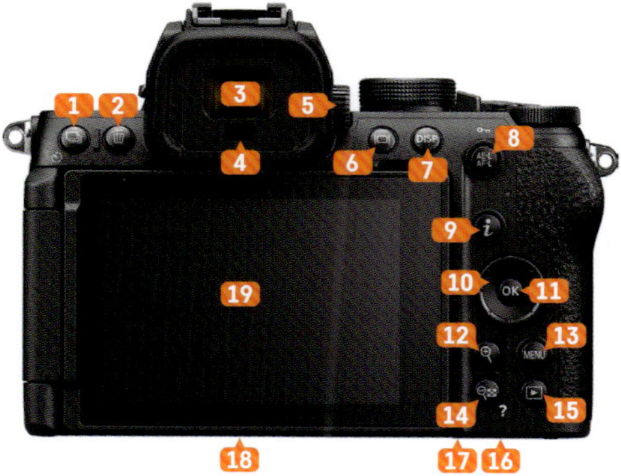

1. **Release Mode Button:** Changes what happens when the shutter release button is pressed.
2. **Delete Button:** Press to delete current image on the LCD.
3. **Viewfinder:** High-resolution electronic viewfinder.
4. **Eye Sensor:** Switches the display from the monitor to the viewfinder when your eye is at viewfinder.
5. **Diopter Adjustment:** Adjust diopter of viewfinder.
6. **Monitor Mode Button:** Changes the monitor display.
7. **DISP Button:** Press this to cycle through display screens.
8. **E/AF Lock/Protect Button:** Exposure/Focus lock/Press during playback to protect the current image.
9. ***i* Button:** Opens a contextual menu that depends on camera mode.
10. **Multi Selector:** Navigates the menus or selects the AF point.
11. **OK Button:** Press to select the current option.
12. **Playback Zoom-In Button:** Zoom in on the current image shown on the LCD.
13. **Menu Button:** Opens and closes camera menu systems.
14. **Playback Button:** Shows the last image taken.
15. **Playback Zoom Out/Thumbnails/Help Button:** Zooms out on current LCD image/Shows images as thumbnails/Press to receive contextual help.
16. **Battery Compartment (On Bottom):** Insert the battery here.
17. **Memory Card Slot (On Bottom):** Insert the memory card here.
18. **Tripod Socket (On Bottom):** Threaded socket for tripod or monopod connection.
19. **Monitor:** Shown closed. Pull it out from top right and rotate it to use.

CAMERA BODY FRONT

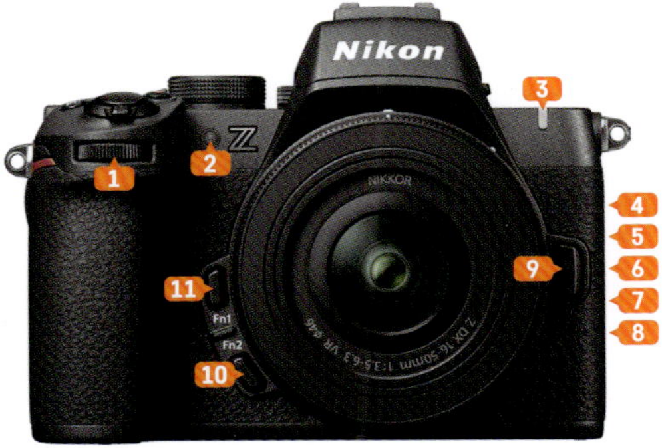

1. **Sub-Command Dial:** Adjusts camera settings.
2. **AF-Assist/Red-Eye Reduction/Self-Timer Lamp:** Illuminates the scene when the lighting is low/Reduces red-eye when using the red-eye reduction modes/Indicates that the self-timer is activated.
3. **REC Lamp:** Will flash when there is an issue with the recording being interrupted: Flashes slowly when you are running out of memory space. Flashes twice when you are running out of battery power. Flashes four times when the camera temperature is rising.
4. **Microphone Connector (Under Side Cover):** Connect external microphone here.
5. **Headphone/Remote Connector (Under Side Cover):** Connect external headphone here.
6. **HDMI Connector (Under Side Cover):** Connect HDMI here.

7. Charge Lamp: Shows when the camera is connected to power and charging.

8. USB Connector (Under Side Cover): Connect USB cable here.

9. Lens Release Button: Press to unlock the lens, then rotate the lens to remove.

10. Fn2 Button: Programmable function button. Default is set for White Balance.

11. Fn1 Button: Programmable function button. Default is set for White Balance.

VIEWFINDER DISPLAY (PHOTO)

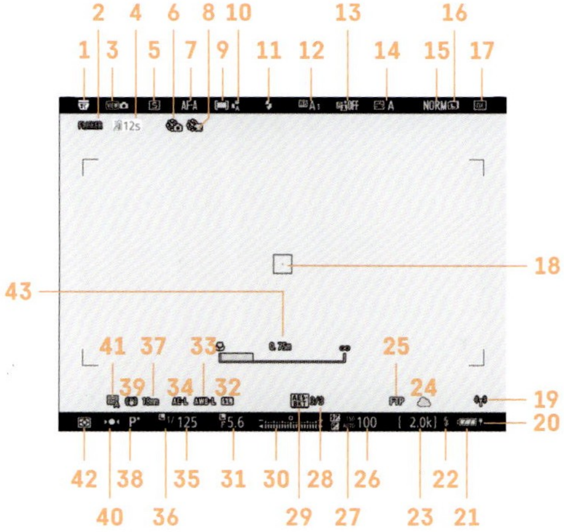

1. **Lens Built-In Teleconverter Enabled Icon:** Shows when the built-in teleconverter is active.
2. **FLICKER Icon:** Shows when flicker reduction is on. Used when shooting under light sources that can cause a flicker, like fluorescent or mercury-vapor lamps.
3. **View Mode:** Shows the current view mode.
4. **Temperature Warning:** Shows when the camera is overheating.
5. **Release Mode:** Shows the current release mode.
6. **Interval Timer Shooting Icon:** Shows when the camera is using Interval Timer Shooting.
7. **Focus Mode:** Shows the current focus mode.
8. **Time-Lapse Video Indicator:** Shows when a time-lapse movie is being made.
9. **AF-Area Mode:** Shows the current AF-Area mode.
10. **Subject Detection Mode:** Shows the current subject detection mode.
11. **Flash Mode:** Shows the current flash mode.
12. **White Balance:** Shows the current White Balance setting.
13. **Active-D Lighting:** Displays the Active-D Lighting status.
14. **Picture Control:** Displays the current Picture Control.
15. **Image Quality:** Shows the current image quality: RAW, RAW+JPEG, or JPEG.
16. **Image Size:** Shows the current image size.
17. **Image Area:** Shows the current image area.
18. **Focus Point:** Shows the selected focus point(s).
19. **Wi-Fi Connection Indicator:** Shows when the camera is connected to Wi-Fi.
20. **USB Power:** Shows when the camera is connected to USB power.
21. **Battery Indicator:** Displays the amount of power left.
22. **Flash Ready:** Shows when the flash is ready to fire.
23. **Number of Exposures Remaining:** Shows the number of photos that can still be taken based on the current settings and the space on the memory card.

24. **Nikon Cloud Connection Status:** Shows when you are connected to the Nikon Cloud.
25. **FTP Connection Status:** Shows when connected via FTP.
26. **ISO Sensitivity:** Shows the current ISO.
27. **ISO/Auto ISO Sensitivity Indicator:** Shows if Auto ISO is enabled.
28. **Number of Shots in Exposure and Flash Bracketing Sequence.**
29. **Exposure/Flash Bracketing Indicator:** Shows when exposure bracketing or flash bracketing is active.
30. **Exposure/Exposure Compensation Indicator:** Shows current exposure and if any exposure compensation is applied.
31. **Aperture:** Shows the current aperture.
32. **FV Lock Indicator:** Shows when the Flash Value is locked.
33. **Auto White Balance Lock:** Shows when White Balance is locked at Auto.
34. **Autoexposure (AE) Lock Indicator:** Shows when the AE lock is active.
35. **Shutter Speed:** Shows the current shutter speed.
36. **Shutter Speed Lock Icon:** Shows when shutter speed is locked.
37. **Focal Length:** Shows current focal length
38. **Shooting Mode:** Shows current shooting mode (P, A, S, M).
39. **Vibration Reduction:** Shows if VR is turned on.
40. **Focus Indicator:** When the middle circle is solid, the subject is in focus.
41. **Shutter Type:** Shows if the electronic shutter or mechanical shutter is selected.
42. **Metering Mode:** Shows the current metering mode.
43. **Distance/Distance Indicator:** Shows the distance between the subject and the camera.

VIEWFINDER DISPLAY (MOVIE)

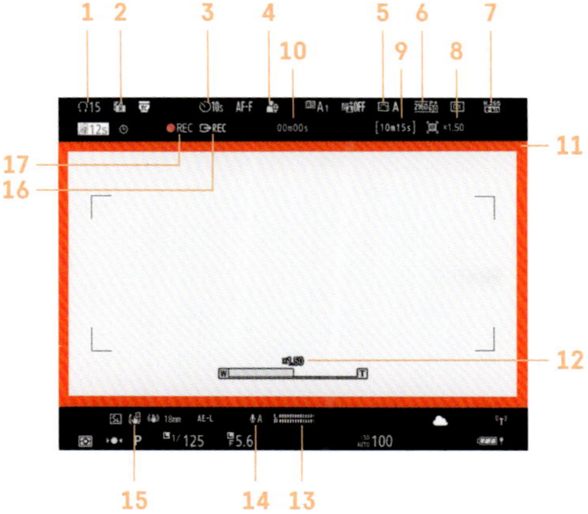

1. Headphone Volume: Shows the current headphone volume level.

2. Zebra Pattern: Shows when active. Can be used to show a zebra pattern in selected tone ranges when shooting video. Menu > Custom Settings > Zebra pattern.

3. Video Self-Timer: Shows when the video self-timer is active.

4. Product Review Mode: Shows when Product Review mode is active. This mode was designed for shooting product review videos. It sets the focus to items close to the camera.

5. Picture Control: Shows the current Picture Control setting.

6. Frame Size/Frame Rate: Shows the current frame size/frame rate.

7. **Video File Type:** Shows the current selected file type.
8. **Hi-Res Zoom Indicator:** Shows when Hi-Res Zoom is active.
9. **Available Recording Time:** The amount of time that can still be recorded.
10. **Length of Recorded Footage Timecode:** Shows the timecode for the current recording. Set the timecode at Menu > Video Recording > Timecode.
11. **Recording Indicator:** The red border indicates that movies are being recorded.
12. **Zoom Position of Hi-Res Zoom:** Shows the Hi-Res zoom setting.
13. **Sound Level:** Shows the current sound levels.
14. **Microphone Sensitivity:** Shows the current microphone sensitivity setting.
15. **Electronic VR Indicator:** Shows when the electronic vibration reduction is turned on.
16. **External Recording Control:** Shows if the camera is recording video to an external recorder via the HDMI port.
17. **Recording Indicator/"No Video" Indicator:** Shows whether a video can be recorded or not.

MONITOR DISPLAY (PHOTO)

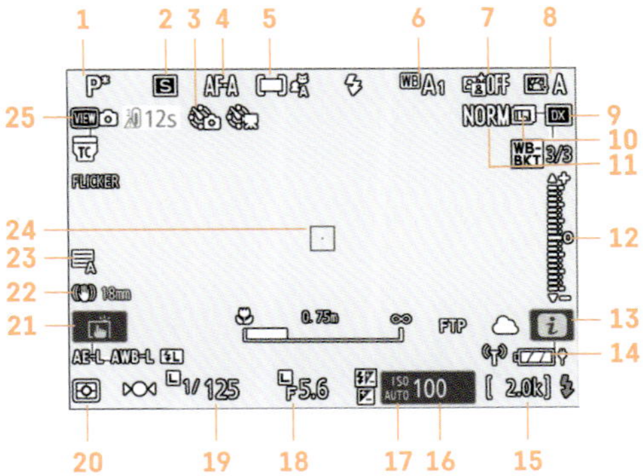

1. **Shooting Mode:** Shows the current shooting mode (P, A, S, M).
2. **Release Mode:** Shows the current release mode.
3. **Interval Timer Photography Indicator:** When flashing, the indicator tells you that the interval timer is active and shooting is in progress.
4. **Focus Mode:** Shows the current focus mode.
5. **AF-Area Mode:** Shows the current AF-Area mode.
6. **White Balance:** Shows current WB setting.
7. **Active-D Lighting:** Displays the Active-D Lighting status.
8. **Picture Control:** Displays the current Picture Control.
9. **Image Area:** Shows the current image area: FX for full frame or DX for cropped sensor.
10. **Image Size:** Shows the current image size.
11. **Image Quality:** Shows the current image quality: RAW, RAW+JPEG, or JPEG.
12. **Exposure/Exposure Compensation Indicator:** Shows the current exposure and if any exposure compensation is applied.

13. *i* **Icon:** Tap the *i* icon to open the *i* menu.
14. **Battery Indicator:** Displays the amount of power left.
15. **Number of Exposures Remaining:** Shows the number of photos that can still be taken based on the current settings and the space on the memory card.
16. **ISO Sensitivity:** Shows the current ISO.
17. **ISO/Auto ISO Sensitivity Indicator:** Shows if Auto ISO is enabled.
18. **Aperture:** Shows the current aperture.
19. **Shutter Speed:** Shows the current shutter speed.
20. **Metering Mode:** Shows the current metering mode.
21. **Touch Shooting:** Shows if touch shooting is enabled.
22. **Vibration Reduction:** Shows if VR is turned on.
23. **Shutter Type:** Shows if the electronic shutter or the mechanical shutter is selected.
24. **Focus Point:** Shows selected focus point(s).
25. **View Mode:** Shows the current view mode.

MONITOR DISPLAY (MOVIE)

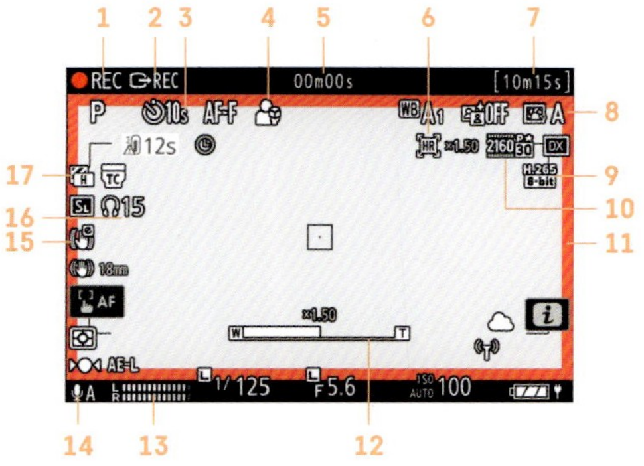

1. **Recording Indicator/"No Video" Indicator:** Shows whether a video can be recorded or not.

2. **External Recording Control:** Shows if the camera is recording video to an external recorder via the HDMI port.

3. **Video Self-Timer:** Shows when the video self-timer is active.

4. **Product Review Mode:** Shows when Product Review mode is active.

5. **Length of Recorded Footage Timecode:** Shows the timecode for the current recording.

6. **Hi-Res Zoom Indicator/Zoom Ratio for Hi-Res Zoom:** Shows when Hi-Res Zoom is active and the current zoom ratio.

7. **Available Recording Time:** Amount of time that can still be recorded.

8. **Picture Control/Tone Mode:** Shows current Picture Control Tone mode setting.

9. **Video File Type:** Shows the current video file type.

10. **Frame Size/Frame Rate:** Shows the current frame size/frame rate.

11. **Recording Indicator:** A red border around the display activates when the camera is recording video.

12. **Zoom Position of Hi-Res Zoom:** Shows the Hi-Res Zoom setting.

13. **Sound Level:** Shows the current sound levels.

14. **Microphone Sensitivity:** Shows the current microphone sensitivity settings.

15. **Electronic VR Indicator:** Shows when the electronic vibration reduction is turned on.

16. **Headphone Volume:** Shows the current headphone volume level.

17. **Zebra Pattern:** Shows when active. Can be used to show a zebra pattern in selected tone ranges when shooting video.

03 ESSENTIAL MODES AND SETTINGS

MODE SHOOTING MODES

Use the mode dial to pick a shooting mode.

AUTO: The camera chooses all the settings.

P (Programmed Auto): The camera sets the shutter speed and aperture based on metering info and the current ISO.

S (Shutter Priority): You set the shutter speed, and camera sets the aperture based on metering info and the current ISO. Shutter speed can be set between 30 sec.–1/4000 sec. When using the electronic front-curtain shutter, the speed is limited to 1/2000 sec.

A (Aperture Priority): You set the aperture, and the camera sets the shutter speed based on metering info and the current ISO. The available range of apertures depends on the lens.

M (Manual): You set both the shutter speed (between 1/4000 sec. and 30 sec.) and the aperture. Set shutter speed to Bulb or Time modes for long exposures. When using the electronic front-curtain shutter, the speed is limited to 1/2000 sec.

U1, U2, and U3 (User Setting): You can assign frequently used settings to three user settings using Setup Menu > Save User Settings.

SCN (Scene): Pick a scene mode by rotating the mode dial to SCN, then rotate the main command dial until the desired scene appears in the monitor.

METERING MODES

Menu > Photo Shooting Menu > Metering

Matrix: The camera uses a wide area of the frame and sets the exposure using the tone distribution, color, composition, and distance to the most realistic exposure.

Center-Weighted: Uses information predominantly from the center of the frame to determine exposure. The size of the area used can be selected using Custom Setting b5 > Center-Weighted Area.

Spot: Uses the area under the current focus point to determine exposure. If Auto-Area AF is in use, the camera uses the center focus point.

Highlight-Weighted: The camera determines exposure to keep detail in the brightest highlights.

EXPOSURE COMPENSATION

Hold the Exposure Compensation button down and rotate the command dial to set a value between –5 (underexposed) and +5 (overexposed) when taking photos (–3 and+3 in video mode).

The default changes to exposure compensation are in increments of 1/3 EV. This can be changed using Custom Setting b2 [EV steps for exposure control].

FOCUS MODES

The focus mode can be selected using the [Focus Mode] item in the *i* menu, Photo Shooting menu, or Video Recording menu.

AF-A (Auto AF): The camera uses AF-S for stationary subjects and AF-C for moving subjects.

AF-S (Single AF): Focus starts when the shutter release is pressed halfway and locks when focus is achieved. Best for stationary subjects.

AF-C (Continuous AF): Focus starts when the shutter release is pressed halfway and continues to focus until photo is taken. Best for moving subjects.

AF-F (Full-Time AF): Only available in Movie mode. Focus tracks subject continuously until the shutter release is pressed halfway.

M (Manual Focus): Focusing is accomplished by turning focusing ring on lens barrel.

AF-AREA MODES

The AF-Area mode can be selected using the [AF-Area Mode/Subj. Detection] item in the *i* menu or the [AF-Area Mode] items in the photo shooting and video recording menus.

Pinpoint AF: Offers a very small, precise AF point that is best for static subjects where the focus is critical on a small part of the subject (AF-S only).

Single-Point AF: A slightly larger focus point than Pinpoint, best for use with stationary subjects.

Dynamic-Area AF (Small, Medium, Large): Uses either the small, medium, or large group of focus points, and if the subject leaves the focus area briefly, the camera uses the surrounding AF points to keep focus locked.

Wide-Area AF (S) (L): Allows the photographer to choose the area used (Small or Large) for the autofocus.

Wide-Area AF (C1) (C2): Allows the photographer to choose the area used for the autofocus using the multi selector to select the height and width.

3D-Tracking: Select the initial focus point and the camera will attempt to track the subject across the frame. AF-C only.

Subject-Tracking AF: Select the initial focus point and the camera will attempt to track the subject across the frame. This is only available in video mode.

Auto-Area AF: Camera automatically detects the subject and decides on the focus area.

RELEASE MODES

Press the Release Mode button and rotate the main command dial to set what happens when you press the shutter release all the way down.

S (Single Frame): Takes a single shot every time the shutter release is pressed.

L (Continuous Low): Takes between 1–5 frames per second (FPS) as long as you press the shutter release.

H (Continuous High): Takes up to 5.6 frames per second (FPS) for as long as you press the shutter release (9.7 FPS in silent mode).

H+ (Continuous High Extended): Takes up to 11 frames per second (FPS) for as long as you press the shutter release (15 FPS in silent mode).

C15: The camera takes photos at 15 frames per second when the shutter release is pressed. Limited to JPEG files.

C30: The camera takes photos at 30 frames per second when the shutter release is pressed. Limited to JPEG files.

Self-Timer: When shutter release is pressed fully, the camera waits a set time before taking the photo.

Note: When using the built-in flash, only one photo is taken each time the shutter release is pressed all the way down even when set to S, L, H, or H+. C15 and C30 modes cannot be used with flash photography.

SHUTTER TYPE

Menu > Custom Setting Menu > Shutter Type

Choose the shutter type used for photography.

Auto: The camera chooses the shutter based on shutter speed. The electronic front-curtain shutter reduces blur caused by camera shake at slower shutter speeds.

Mechanical Shutter: The camera uses the mechanical shutter for all photos.

Electronic Front-Curtain Shutter: The camera uses the electronic shutter for all photos. Top shutter speed is limited to 1/2000 second.

WHITE BALANCE

White balance can be adjusted using the [White Balance] item in the *i* menu, Photo Shooting menu, or Video Recording menu. At default settings, white balance can be selected by holding the Fn1 button and rotating the main command dial. The selected option is displayed by an icon in the shooting display.

The **A (Auto)** setting is best for most situations. White balance can be set to shift colors warmer, cooler, or keep them accurate. Other settings are all matched to different lighting types. For truest colors, pick the type of lighting being used to illuminate scene.

IMAGE AREA/QUALITY/SIZE

Menu > Photo Shooting Menu > Choose Image Area

DX (24x16): Camera uses an image area of 23.5×15.7 mm (DX format). To calculate the approximate focal length of the lens in 35mm format, multiply by 1.5.

1:1 (16x16): Photos are recorded using a square aspect ratio.

16:9 (24x14): Photos are recorded with wide "letterbox" aspect ratio.

Menu > Photo Shooting Menu > Image Quality

RAW (NEF): The RAW data from the image sensor is recorded each time a photo is taken.

RAW (NEF) + JPEG/HEIF: The camera saves two files each time the shutter button is pressed: a RAW file and a JPEG or HEIF file. The size for photographs recorded in JPEG and HEIF formats (not NEF (RAW)) can be specified as [Large], [Medium], and [Small]. NEF (RAW) pictures are recorded as [Large] setting.

JPEG/HEIF: The camera saves a JPEG or HEIF file each time the shutter button is pressed. You can decide the quality of the JPEG (Fine, Normal, or Basic).

Menu > Photo Shooting Menu > Image Size

Choose the size of your images (Large, Medium, or Small). All RAW (NEF) photos are recorded in the large size.

04 OTHER HELPFUL SETTINGS

PICTURE CONTROLS

The Picture Control system allows you to share image processing settings (sharpening, contrast, brightness, saturation, and hue) among compatible devices and software. The following Picture Controls are available:

Picture Control: Standard Picture Controls provided with the camera.

Creative Picture Control: Creative Picture Controls provided with the camera.

Picture Control (HLG): Picture Controls provided with the camera. They are selected via [Set Picture Control (HLG)] in the Photo Shooting menu when [Tone Mode] in the Photo Shooting menu is set to [HLG] in photo mode.

Custom Picture Control: Picture Controls created with the camera or NX Studio computer software. To create Custom Picture Controls with the camera, use [Manage Picture Control] in the photo shooting or video recording menu.

Cloud Picture Control: Picture Controls provided by the Nikon Imaging Cloud service. They can be downloaded and imported to the camera as Picture Controls.

Select Picture Controls by pressing the **Picture Control** button and then using the left and right buttons on the multi selector. Press OK to make your selection. You can pick from the following: **A (AUTO)**, **SD (Standard)**, **NL (Neutral)**, **VI (Vivid)**, **MC (Monochrome)**, **FM (Flat Monochrome)**, **DM (Deep Tone Monochrome)**, **PT (Portrait)**, **RP (Rich Tone Portrait)**, **LS (Landscape)**, **FL (Flat)**, **01–20 (Creative Picture Control)**, **C1-C9 (Custom Picture Control)**, and **1-9 (Cloud Picture Control)**.

You can modify the Picture Controls by pressing the Picture Control button and using the left and right buttons on the multi selector to pick a Picture Control, then press the down arrow on the multi selector. You can now use the up and down arrows on the multi selector to choose the setting to adjust, then use the left and right arrows on the multi selector to adjust each setting. Press the OK button to save changes.

The following can be adjusted, but not all adjustments are available for all Picture Controls: **Effect Level**, **Quick Sharp**, **Sharpness**, **Mid-range Sharpening**, **Clarity, Contrast**,

Highlights, **Shadows**, **Brightness**, **Saturation**, **Hue**, **Filter Effects**, and **Toning** (there is also a Toning setting for Creative Picture Controls).

Monochrome images can have a yellow, orange, red, or green filter applied.

The only options when the photo/video selector is set to B&W are **Monochrome**, **Flat Monochrome**, and **Deep Tone Monochrome**.

FLASH MODES

Set the Flash mode using the *i* menu or the Photo Shooting menu. The options available will depend on the shooting mode.

Fill Flash: The flash fires with each shot. When using P or A shooting mode, the camera uses a shutter speed between 1/60–1/200 sec. (1/60–1/4000 sec. when Auto FP High-Speed Sync is selected).

Red-Eye Reduction: The flash will fire or the camera's red-eye reduction lamp will illuminate prior to the main flash firing, reducing the red-eye. Not good for moving subjects.

Slow Sync: Flash is used in conjunction with slower shutter speeds to allow ambient light into the photo. Only available in P and A shooting modes.

Slow Sync and Red-Eye Reduction: Combines the red-eye reduction lamp and slow sync for better portraits when you want ambient light in the photo. Only available in P and A shooting modes.

Rear-Curtain Sync: Flash fires at the end of the exposure, creating more natural-looking light trails if the subject is moving.

Auto: The flash fires automatically when the subject is too dark or backlit.

Auto + Red-Eye Reduction: Combines the Auto flash functionality with red-eye reduction. Only available when the shooting mode is set to one of the SCN modes or Auto shooting mode.

Auto Slow Sync: Uses a slower shutter speed when the flash fires. Only available in the Night Portrait scene mode.

Auto Slow Sync + Red-Eye Reduction: Uses slow sync and red-eye reduction when the flash fires. Only available in the Night Portrait scene mode.

Flash Off: Flash does not fire.

COLOR SPACE

Menu > Photo Shooting Menu > Color Space

sRGB: Smaller color space. Best when images are used directly from camera.

Adobe RGB: Larger color space. Best when images will be edited with post-processing software.

HIGHLIGHT DISPLAY (BLINKIES)

Playback Menu > Playback Display Options, select Highlights

Shows pure-white areas as blinking highlights on playback. Useful to know if areas are being overexposed.

NOISE REDUCTION

Menu > Photo Shooting Menu > Long Exposure NR

Reduces noise in images with shutter speeds of 1 second or longer. Doubles time needed to save image to memory card.

Menu > Photo Shooting Menu > High ISO NR

Reduces noise in images taken at high ISO settings. Use Normal for default, Low for less noise reduction, and High for more noise reduction. You can also select Off, which still might apply some noise reduction, but it is less than Low.

VIBRATION REDUCTION

Menu > Photo Shooting Menu > Vibration Reduction

On (Normal): Used for vibration reduction when shooting stationary subjects.

SPT (Sports): Used for shooting moving subjects.

Off: Vibration reduction is turned off.

Vibration reduction will depend on the lens that is attached to the camera.

ISO/AUTO ISO

Hold the ISO button and rotate the main command dial to set the ISO.

Turn Auto ISO on/off by pressing the ISO button and rotating the sub-command dial. The maximum ISO used in the Auto ISO mode is set at Photo Shooting Menu > ISO Sensitivity Setting.

DISP BUTTON

Press the DISP button to cycle through up to five customizable displays.

The items shown can be selected at Menu > Custom Setting Menu > [Custom Monitor Shooting Display]. Highlight Display 2 through Display 5, and press OK to select or deselect.

The selected displays will be shown when the DISP button is pressed. Display 1 cannot be deselected.

To select what is shown on each display, select Display 1 through 4 (Display 5 is the information display and cannot be customized) and press right on the multi selector. Now select what you want to see on the displays.

SIMPLE (Basic shooting info): Shows shooting mode, shutter speed, aperture, and other basic information.

DETAIL (Detailed shooting info): Shows focus mode, AF-Area mode, WB, and other detailed information.

Touch Controls: Shows the options that can be accessed by touch, including touch AF and the *i* menu.

Virtual Horizon: Shows a virtual horizon.

Histogram: Displays the RGB histogram.

Framing Grid: Displays a grid that is customizable at Menu > Custom Settings Menu > d Shooting / Display > 18 [Grid Type].

Center Indicator: Displays crosshairs at the center of the frame.

Center-Weighted Area: A 6- or 8-mm circle is added to the center of the shooting display when the metering mode is set to center-weighted.

ACTIVE D-LIGHTING

Photo Shooting Menu > Active D-Lighting

Used to help preserve detail that can be lost in both the darkest and brightest parts of a high-contrast image. You can set the strength to **Auto**, **Extra High**, **High**, **Normal**, or **Low**, or you can turn Active D-Lighting off.

Note: This feature can cause image issues such as banding and noise at higher ISO settings.

BKT AUTO BRACKETING

Menu > Photo > Photo Shooting Menu > Auto Bracketing

Auto Bracketing is used to take a set of images where exposure, flash power, white balance, or Active D-Lighting is changed slightly between each frame. You can set the camera to whichever option you would like to bracket.

Exposure (AE) & Flash: Changes the exposure and the flash power.

Exposure (AE): Changes the exposure.

Flash: Changes the flash power.

WB: Changes the white balance.

ADL: Changes the amount of the Active D-Lighting applied.

Select the number of shots and the time increment between photos (with ADL, select an amount).

WIRELESS CONNECTION (SNAPBRIDGE)

Use the Nikon SnapBridge app on your smartphone or tablet to connect the Z50 II to the device.

Allows for wireless downloading of images and remote control of camera.

05 STEP-BY-STEP SHOOTING INSTRUCTIONS

MULTIPLE EXPOSURES

Create in-camera multiple exposures from 2 to 10 RAW (NEF) files:

1. Select Photo Shooting Menu > Multiple Exposure Mode, and press right on the multi selector.
2. Choose the Multiple Exposure mode:

   On (series): Takes multiple exposures until Off is selected.

   On (single): Takes one multiple exposure.

   Off: Turns multiple exposures off.
3. Select Number of Shots to combine.
4. Pick the Overlay mode:

   Add: The images are combined without any modification.

   Average: Before the images are combined, the gain for each image is divided by the total number of images to create a proper exposure.

Lighten: The camera uses only lightest pixels of each image to create an overall light image.

Darken: The camera uses only darkest pixels of each image to create an overall dark image.

5. Choose whether to keep the individual images or just the multiple exposure by selecting Save Individual Pictures (RAW) and choosing On or Off, then pressing OK.

6. Choose whether to view the progress in the display by selecting Overlay Shooting and choosing On or Off, then pressing OK.

7. Choose the Select First Exposure (RAW) option, then press right on the multi selector. Highlight the image using the multi selector and press OK.

Take the selected number of photos and the camera will combine them into a single JPEG image.

HDR HDR

Combine two images to reduce the contrast and improve tonal range:

1. Select Photo Shooting Menu > HDR Overlay, and press right on the multi selector.

2. Choose HDR Mode and press right on the multi selector to shoot either a series (On [Series]) or just a single occurrence (On [Single Photo]), or select Off, which stops HDR shooting.

3. For HDR Strength, choose one of the following: Auto, Extra High, High, Normal, or Low.

4. Choose whether to keep the individual exposures (Save Individual Pictures [RAW]).

5. Press the shutter release button once to take the two photos that end up as a single HDR JPEG.

If the camera is set to Series, it will continue to take HDR images until you open the menu and change that setting to Off. If the camera is set to Single Photo, it will turn HDR off after you take the first HDR photo.

TIME-LAPSE VIDEOS

Create a time-lapse video in-camera:

1. Select Photo Shooting Menu > Time-Lapse Video, and press right on the multi selector.

2. Select the Interval, which is the time between each photo. Set in minutes and seconds.

3. Select the Shooting Time, which is how long to shoot (up to 23 hours and 59 minutes).

4. Choose whether or not you want to use Exposure Smoothing. When On, the camera automatically tries to smooth any big changes in the exposure.

5. Choose whether to use the electronic shutter: When on, the electronic shutter is used, and the sound of the shutter can be set using the volume setting.

6. Choose the Video File Type: H.265 8-Bit (MOV) or H.264 8-Bit (MP4).

7. Choose the Frame Size/Frame Rate.

8. Turn Interval Priority on or off. On ensures that frames shot in P or A mode will use the set interval even if that creates an underexposed image.

9. Select whether or not the camera needs to focus between each shot.

10. Select Start and press OK.

INTVL INTERVAL TIMER PHOTOGRAPHY

Set the camera to take a series of photos over a period of time:

1. Select Photo Shooting Menu > Interval Timer Shooting, and press right on the multi selector.

2. Set the Start option to begin in 3 seconds (choose Now) or at least 1 minute in the future (choose Day/Time).

3. Set the interval between photos (Hours/Minutes/Seconds).

4. Set the number of intervals and the number of shots per interval (Intervals x Shots/Interval).

5. Turn Exposure Smoothing on or off.

6. Choose whether or not to use the electronic shutter. When on, the electronic shutter is used, and the sound of the shutter can be set using the volume setting.

7. Turn Interval Priority on or off. When on, photos shot in P or A mode will be taken at the chosen interval; when off, the camera will use the shutter speed to achieve proper exposure even if that is longer than the selected interval.

8. Choose if the camera focuses between each shot.

9. Choose Options to set AE Bracketing (set the number of shots and the change in exposure [Increment]) or Time-Lapse Video (choose the settings for Video File Type, Frame Size/Frame Rate, and Destination). Or set to Off.

10. Select the Starting Storage Folder if the image numbering needs to be reset.

11. Select Start and press OK.

FOCUS SHIFT SHOOTING

The camera takes a series of photos, starting with the selected focus point and moving toward infinity. The starting point should be slightly in front of the subject. The camera needs to be in the same position until shooting ends. Before using Focus Shift, choose a focus mode (AF-A, AF-S, or AF-C) and a release mode other than Self-Timer or High-Speed Frame Capture +.

1. Select Photo Shooting Menu > Focus Shift Shooting, and press right on the multi selector.

2. Select the number of shots (up to 300). Choose more than you think you need, especially for macro subjects.

3. Choose the amount the focus distance changes between shots using the left and right buttons on the multi selector. Lower settings will ensure more of the final image is in focus.

4. Choose the interval between photos. If using a flash, make sure you leave enough time for the flash to fully recharge between photos.

5. Enable or disable First-Frame Exposure Lock. Off is recommended when you know the exposure isn't going to change and On is recommended when shooting landscapes and other subjects where you don't have control over the light.

6. Choose whether to use the electronic shutter: When on, the electronic shutter is used, and the sound of the shutter can be set using the volume setting.

7. Choose whether or not the focus position returns to its starting position at the end of each sequence. On is recommended if you plan on taking multiple sequences of the same subject.

8. Select the Starting Storage Folder if the image numbering needs to be reset.

9. Select Start and press OK.

06 TYPICAL SHOOTING SCENARIOS

SHOOTING SCENARIO
PORTRAIT

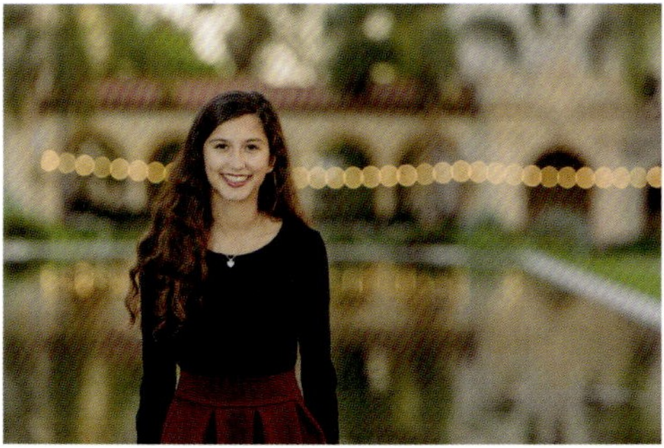

KEY PRINCIPLES

- The key to a portrait like this is shallow depth of field. Shoot in **APERTURE PRIORITY** mode and start with the lowest aperture your lens offers (such as **f/2.8** or **f/4**).
- Remember to **focus on the eyes**.

- If the image is too dark or too light, use **EXPOSURE COMPENSATION** to adjust the brightness level.
- If the image is blurry from a slow shutter speed, **raise the ISO** to increase your sensor's sensitivity to light, thus allowing for a faster shutter speed.
- Remember to use a **focal length of 50mm or greater** so that you don't distort your subject's face.

SHOOTING SCENARIO
GROUP PORTRAIT

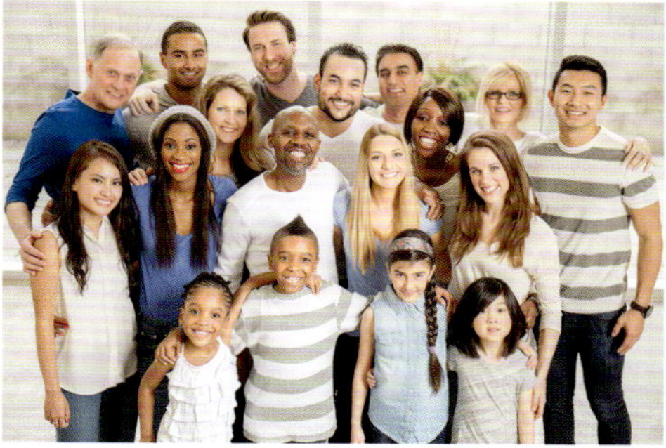

KEY PRINCIPLES

- To get everyone in focus, you need a deep depth of field. Shoot in **APERTURE PRIORITY** mode and set the aperture between **f/8–f/16**.
- **Focus on the person in the middle of the group.** Check focus by using the Zoom In button to view it at 100% and check faces in the front and back rows. If anyone is out of focus, use a smaller aperture for deeper depth of field.
- Use **MATRIX METERING** to account for the light in the entire scene.
- **Arrange the group so they can all see you** (and you can see them).
- Use **EXPOSURE COMPENSATION** if the image is too bright or too dark.
- If the image is blurry, **raise the ISO** to allow the camera to use a faster shutter speed.

SHOOTING SCENARIO

LANDSCAPE

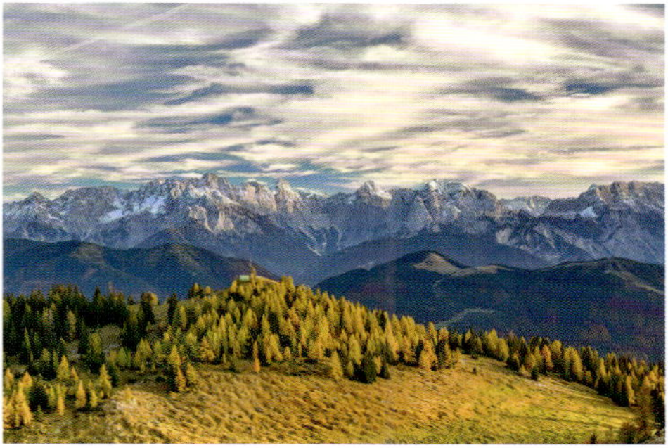

KEY PRINCIPLES

- Shoot in **APERTURE PRIORITY** to control depth of field. Start with **f/16** to ensure deep depth of field.
- **Use a tripod** to eliminate camera movement.
- Use **MATRIX METERING** mode and **SINGLE AUTOFOCUS (AF-S)** focus mode.
- **Set the ISO to a low setting (100–200)** to avoid any digital noise.

- Shoot in **RAW** so that you have the most available information when editing later.
- Consider **BRACKETING** your exposures.

SHOOTING SCENARIO
FREEZE ACTION

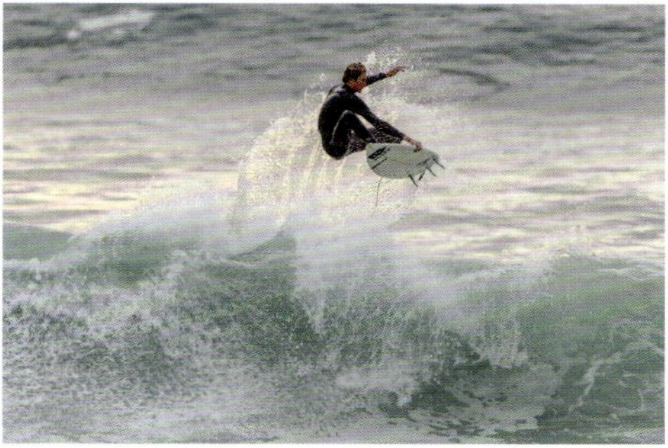

KEY PRINCIPLES

- Use **SHUTTER PRIORITY** mode and set the shutter speed to a value that will freeze the action. The appropriate shutter speed depends on your subject and its movement, but could be anywhere between **1/500–1/4000 sec**. Use the mechanical shutter to get the higher shutter speeds.

- Use **CONTINUOUS AUTOFOCUS (AF-C)** so the camera keeps focusing as the subject moves.
- If the image is dark or blurry, **raise the ISO** or try **AUTO ISO** to automatically have the camera adjust the ISO as needed.

SHOOTING SCENARIO
SHOWING MOTION—PANNING

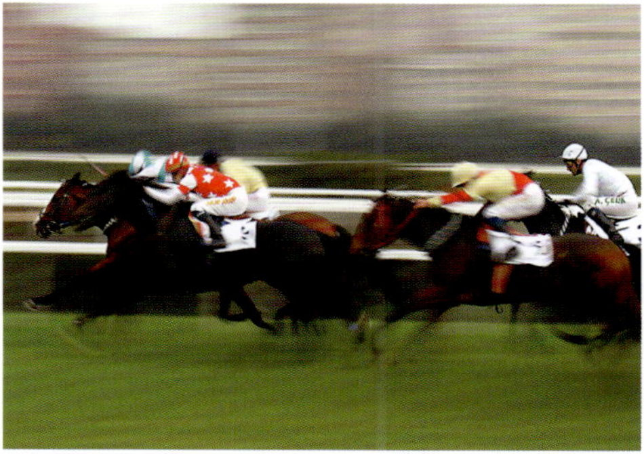

KEY PRINCIPLES

- Shoot in **SHUTTER PRIORITY** mode and use a slow enough shutter speed to allow for the subject to move during the exposure.

- **Follow the subject** across the frame as you shoot.
- Use **CONTINUOUS AUTOFOCUS (AF-C)** and **3D-Tracking AF** to help keep the subject in focus.

SHOOTING SCENARIO
LOW-LIGHT ACTION

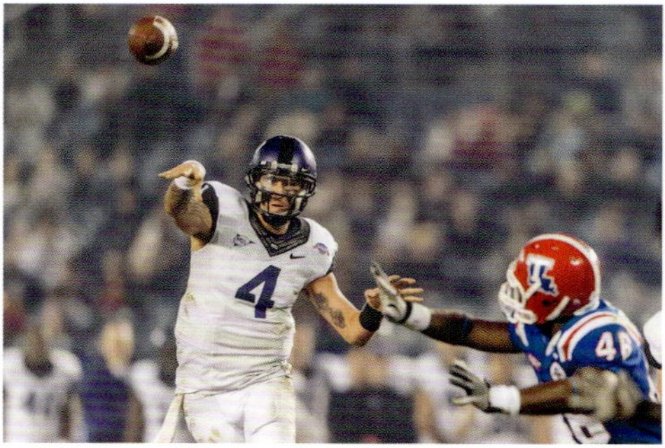

KEY PRINCIPLES

- Shoot in **APERTURE PRIORITY** mode and use a wide aperture such as **f/2.8** or **f/4**.
- Use **SPOT METERING** and meter on the subject's face.
- Use **CONTINUOUS AUTOFOCUS (AF-C)** and a single AF point.

- **Set the ISO to 1600 or higher**, depending on the amount of available light.
- If the image is blurry, **increase the ISO** to allow for a faster shutter speed.

SHOOTING SCENARIO
LONG EXPOSURE

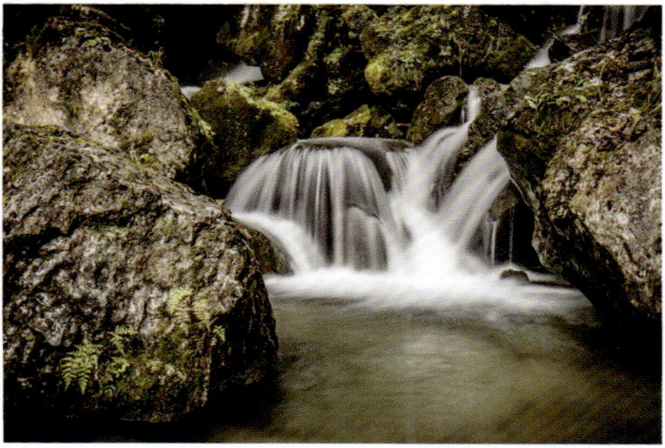

KEY PRINCIPLES

- Use **MANUAL** shooting mode, which allows you to use the **BULB** or **TIME** setting for long exposures.
- **Use a tripod** to keep the camera stable.

- Use the **SINGLE AUTOFOCUS (AF-S)** focus mode, or try manual focus if the camera is having a hard time locking on focus.
- **Use a low ISO (100–400)** and **shoot RAW** to ensure a high-quality file.
- **Use a remote** with a lock to avoid touching (shaking) the camera, such as the Nikon MC-DC3 remote release cord.

SHOOTING SCENARIO
MACRO/CLOSE-UP

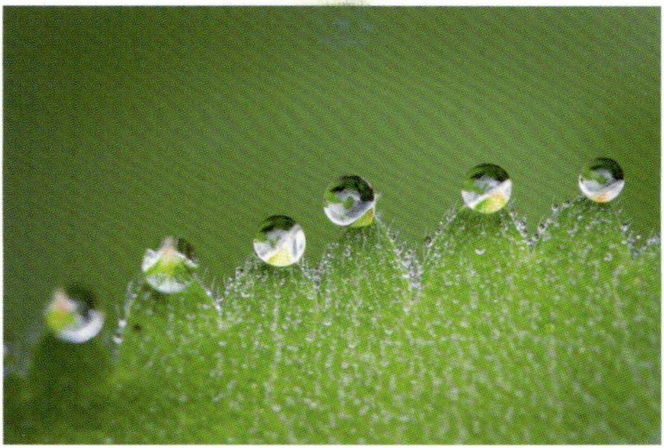

KEY PRINCIPLES

- Shoot in **APERTURE PRIORITY** mode and **use a small aperture** to ensure you achieve enough depth of field (this image was shot at f/13).
- Use **MATRIX METERING** to analyze the light in the entire frame.
- A **tripod** is very useful for keeping the camera steady.

SHOOTING SCENARIO
VIDEO RECORDING/VLOGGING

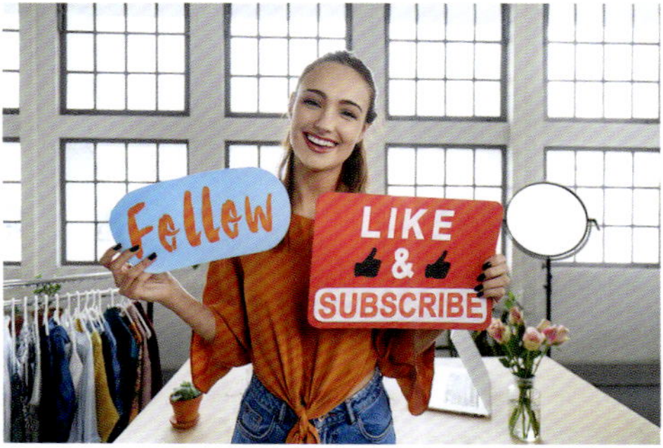

KEY PRINCIPLES

- Use a **shallow depth of field** to keep the viewers' attention on the subject. A **wide aperture** will keep the subject in focus while having the area in front of and behind the subject fall out of focus.
- Use **24 fps** for a more cinematic look.
- Set the **shutter speed** to **twice the frame rate**, or as close as you can get. If using 24 fps, the shutter speed should be 1/50 (or 1/60) second.
- Use an **external microphone** for better sound. The Rode VideoMic GO II is a great starter microphone.
- Keep the camera stable with a **tripod or gimble**. Smooth footage looks more professional.
- Remember to leave a second of two of nothing at the beginning and end of your video clips—this will make them much easier to edit later.